THE PORTAGE POETRY SERIES

SERIES TITLES

PRAISE FOR

The Vinegar in Our Hearts

Jesse DeLong is writing some of the most complex and exciting love poetry out there right now, and *The Vinegar in Our Hearts* raises the bar as to what a love poem can do both in form and content. DeLong's poetry in this new collection manages to be both inventive and insightful, experimental without ever surrendering its heart.

—*TRAMPOLINE POETRY*

Reader, the book you hold is made of poems which make a novel constantly unmaking itself; an (unfinished) essay on "Unrealistic Conceptions of Love in Malcolm Lowry's *Under the Volcano*"; and a letter from a former lover to a formerly beloved. Much of the book's matter is compressed into that most compact and demanding of fixed forms, the triolet, which, in Jesse DeLong's deft and artful hands, acts as a prism, refracting and defamiliarizing language, thought, and feeling, and revealing the mind to itself as "a collage/ different than exists in the known universe." Also revealed: the heart, here a vessel for vinegar, that astringent, if flavorful, if no longer intoxicating, remnant of love. Maximalist and minimalist, brilliant and tender, *The Vinegar in Our Hearts* resists the constraining artifice of closure, offering instead "silence and solitude not as an emptiness, but as a fullness of self." Take it as it is offered: in kind.

—BRAD RICHARD
author of *Turned Earth*

Jesse DeLong's *The Vinegar in Our Hearts* reminds me of why I fell in love with traditional forms. DeLong commits to the triolet form for almost the entirety of this collection, and over time, language gets more slippery, slides right through our fingers. In each 8-line snapshot, DeLong bends language as far as it will go, repurposing and rejuvenating language, injecting emotional weight into broken and rearranged fragments, concentrating philosophical wanderings into throat-searing shots of clarity. And between each beautiful burst of language, a choreographed quiet, the "silence an oven our heads are closed in."

—TAYLOR BYAS
author of *Resting Bitch Face*

In this contemplative and stirring collection, Jesse DeLong uses the constrictive triolet to tell an expansive story of both loss and possibility. These poems are mirrors held up to themselves. "To name anything is to neutralize it enough, / the marker for measuring nostalgia," his speaker sings, and it's in this naming that the world becomes a place of possibility and promise, with each repeated line offering an opportunity to reshape the world as we know it. This is a formal book of wild and epic proportions.

—ADAM CLAY
author of *Circle Back*

The Vinegar in Our Hearts

triolets

Jesse DeLong

CORNERSTONE PRESS
UNIVERSITY OF WISCONSIN-STEVENS POINT

Cornerstone Press, Stevens Point, Wisconsin 54481
Copyright © 2026 Jesse DeLong
www.uwsp.edu/cornerstone

Printed in the United States of America.

Library of Congress Control Number: 2026930441
ISBN: 978-1-968148-33-1

Cornerstone Press titles are produced in courses and internships offered by the
Department of English at the University of Wisconsin–Stevens Point.

DIRECTOR & PUBLISHER
Dr. Ross K. Tangedal

EXECUTIVE EDITORS
Jeff Snowbarger, Freesia McKee

EDITORIAL DIRECTOR
Brett Hill

SENIOR EDITORS
Paige Biever, Reilly Crous

PRESS STAFF
Lillian Kulbeck, McKenna Bartel, Gwen Goetter, Allison Lange, Sophie
McPherson, Sam Bjork, Andrew Bryant

To my former classmates—for helping me find my form again and anew.

ALSO BY JESSE DeLONG:

The Amateur Scientist's Notebook

CONTENTS

1.

2.

3.

4.

1.

Gong goes the bell-jar goes the gong.

What's the use of escaping from ourselves.
All anyone needs is to feel like he is hungry.
I sit at the kitchen table. Sun algaes the room. Bird tells
me what to use when escaping from ourselves.
In the scarred tissue of my sternum, I feel it again, bells
ringing in a town no one resides in. Run & see
what it is you feed on. Escaping from ourselves
is all anyone needs. To feel like she, too, is hungry.

The sun is a blister on the sky.

Let's see what this feels like, this blind point of hunger.
At the center is a cold, original pleasure.
Bird & I, tourists of June, toting oversized umbrellas
to see what it feels like. This blind point. Hunger
is to simply nub bone-near in flesh, but feel younger
than the one you run shadowed in the sun beside. Bird
measuring what the blind point feels like. Let's hunger
originally. Cold in the sun—the center of pleasure.

Gravitating onto the couch, Bird and I both pretend the eros, bittersweet, and between us, must be dealt with.

Here's to your love. What's my name? She pushes
these toward him (a Grecian urn, the spines of magnets)
along with a saucer flush with salt & some smushed
plums. Here's to you. Love it. What my name pushes
against the dryness of lips. The air in the room: squished
peppers, dustings of salt. Something edible for a bit.
Here it is, he says, to his love. What? My name. She pushes
toward him. He withdraws, yearning. Bodies meaty magnets.

As Bird is quilling—like feathers from a boiled chicken—some grass, a hawk offers its shadow instead. Light returns to her face, and she emits an omen.

Who rose in the morning & disappeared in the sun?
Two months lean gently into each other, enduring the dust.
Far off, earth charred—a thunderclap. The shadows of rain run
on those who rise. The morning disappears beneath pines
when we give up eating from the white dish filled with plums.
Each of us has something to offer, but won't, though we must,
suffer for the ones who rose to confront sweat, sun-
stained & sooted, those of the lost hundreds. Those few enduring.

Sitting on a hill overlooking Tuscaloosa, the view we hoped for—what, exactly?—turns out to be streetlights in a dirty string over the valley. As if someone, too lazy, like me, to take down the Christmas lights, stumbled outside, post-storm, a June morning, and saw the lights strewn on the grass, still lit, though most of the bulbs busted, and didn't bother, because of how their light is subject to the sun's light, picking them up.

Smashed bits of glass, the trials of an afternoon—
now only night, heat, the press of knucklebone.
The light of the sky, as if to make room, overwhelms
with its bright bits of glass. An event that, after
it happens, is stripped away. Memory is
the shadow of someone in an alley as we walk by.
After you, trembling—the smashed bits of your life.
Only now, the night pressed. So often, a knucklebone.

It hasn't been dry for days. The grass, thick, wavers like a nervous tic. The treeline a horizon birds buoy. When a hawk capsizes, Bird and I spread an old quilt and picnic there.

Sky, a glass of water poured. Bits of mold-rot broken off.
The world eddied out in seepage, lungs sopped, pupils immersed
in salt. Bird, too, lies down, drought-anxious, in the grass. A tideline
of dandelions at her toes. Small hawk, sunk. Broken off
wind tattering into grass. What's expected, then, of my post-
uring? Could I, staggering, womb-driven, to earth,
rowboat these drowsy hours where bits of mold
are scrapped out for water-rot, rain-thirst broken off since birth?

The way grass snaps over in a crop circle, the trees look around the tornado-hit lake. Someone's basement, like the split belly of a fish, is exposed, showing its canned peas, acorn squash, lima beans. Several of us are left with only the hallways of our houses. Huddled under a pillow in the bathtub. A year later, there is still a dumpster, red as a siren, in the lake.

Unacceptable—what a person is asked to endure
in a life. Maybe it's not to be, not really.
Even the smallest task, at the end, becomes difficult
to ask of a person, who is, after all, an unacceptable
amount of flesh. Somewhere, in the bowels—a self.
Or possibly not even that. Maybe, like a lichen, only
an illusion of wholeness. What's endured—a person is.
A life—not to be, but rather, to not be nothing.

Why I prefer "endure" instead of "endear."

The estrangement of man is unconquerable. Even
god, sick of hallelujahs, cannot conquer it.
So why not endure these in Bird: flesh, saliva, semen,
a cycle of transgressions so earthly even god wouldn't squander it.
But she demands more, a sponge wrung. There's no reason
to hunger like starving angels—that rustic pitch
of bodies endeared. Whether this man, all air & silt, is conquerable
believing god, lungs full of used-up light, cannot conjure such hymns.

Slumped against the front bumper of my
Mercury Comet, I hold a map the way you'd
expect someone like me to. I feel the way the
weather does—windless. Everywhere, miles of
Bigsky grass an eighth a tank of gas won't cover.
As I glance at the map, my finger rests on a town
whose name sounds faintly recognizable, like a
voice underwater.

At least on the edge—the town, the sunflowers
among the garbage—it's much, much too late
to pretend we can withstand, like a sun-dial, the hours.
At the edge of town, sun flowers the least. Whose
entire life could be grey, but he still believes in yellow?
It takes someone stronger than me not to hate,
at least, myself. Driven to the edge,
among the garbage—it's much, much, much.

When the pond water is too brown to see the birds,
behind you in the sky, coming and coming and
coming.

Was it some figment of himself, he who had once
enjoyed such a simple healthy stupid thing as blind luck?
He pointed to runnels of sky, a wilderness of marsh, blunt
birds: simply scriptures unwritten on the sun. He, who had once
swam in sweatpants through trout-brown water, sung
of gnat-wings, morels, such small drums of the fucked-
up choir—some figment of himself, he who had once
enjoyed such. Simply healthy, stupid. His life, a tumor benign.

After withdrawing a curtain of marsh grass, the Admiral and I emerge on red clay. He removes a flask from the breast pocket of his flannel jacket. As he drinks, sunlight careens off its metal casing. He offers it to me, filtering air in lungs, and I notice that a duck is rising and falling among the cattails, which, somehow, are not moving.

Something of Earth's gravity, & the dream
life of plants. He whispers in my ear,
the Admiral, someone who has felt too often
the earth's gravity. So wrong, ripple-lost. Dream,
Bird, a head full of curls. What small scene
of my life did you enter? What atomic furl,
something like the Earth's? Or a dreamed gravity?
Cattails, he whispers, halitosis on tongue, break now.

As if the runnel is a river, and the wedding dress
a baby sent on a reed-woven carriage, the dress
drapes over the storm grate. Bird lifts its fabric,
the yellowish lace flapping as water gurgles into
the opening. She leers up at me. This is where
she will nest: the sun half-clotted by clouds.

The way you feel—a tooth sensitive to saliva.
"Yes," Bird says, "I do." Everything else is a squat
little plot of land that the wind begins to rip up.
Feeling the way you salivate, Bird, is sensitive. Too
much like a mirror facing a mirror. Fingers, stinging
because the blood is too constricted, seem sensitive.
They are really dulled by the way you feel
everything. Or else. "I say," she does. "Yes."

Silence honeycombs my throat. And so Bird, who believes communication is shaped in the cadence of response, buries a broom handle into a wasp's nest, parchment grey and plastered to our porch awning. The bees—roiled silt—swarm. We wait, not to see whether they'll rage, no, no, but whether, after a month or so, they'll return.

The hell they want? Bird was saying. Why,
she scarcely knew, a month later, to me.
Such time is resolved in the present. Her & I
getting the hell we wanted. Bird saying, why,
lonely bee, must you do this to us? Together
a couple of wasps whose nest disjarred from tree.
To hell, I said. Why do you want it, Bird?
She knew scarcity this month. Sometime later: me.

From the tear-shaped light of the match, to the globulous light of the firefly, to the voluminous and emptying light of the moon, to the early light of the north star, and back, as always, to the fireflies, a group of them now, sifting in the air over the grass— see, there, their own constellations.

These are different kinds of knowledge.
It is quite new, Bird says, what cannot be held
there. The mind, I say, is a collage
different than what exists in the known universe.
To grasp one thing & then it's opposite. A mirage
your whole life is. Stability in the unstable. What is felt,
Bird says, is different than the kinds of knowledge
that can be held. Quite. What cannot, now, be new?

The Admiral finds an old violin on the pavement behind a grocery store. Its strings have been strummed so much they drape. All afternoon, he tries to play it.

One sees that music has its place
in thought, but hardly as yet in language.
Bird, please, don't look so disgraced.
Music has won. See. Its place
is not with us—grammar can't mimic bass,
drums, love, a heartbeat, anguish.
One sees that. Music has it. Placed
in thought, but hardly. Its own only language.

The Admiral, sucking on a cough drop to hide the smell, lets me in his front door. "Brother," he says and sits on the only chair at the kitchen table. He is wearing a white shirt, browned from sweat like he's been sleeping in it for a week—the way the air smells in Alabama. The scar on his left arm shows. When he raises his head, he draws the muscles of his face up, looking, briefly, like some horrible figure on an Etch-A-Sketch. The phone rings. "Don't," he says into the receiver, "do anything about that ditch. Just don't touch the leaves." He switches the phone from right to left. "If you do, all you'll hear," he is yelling now, "is zing zing zing and you'll be leaving in a body bag."

He is alone with his own revulsions.
Subdue, he does, his appetites, but occasionally
concedes. It's as if an outside propulsion
alone becomes his own. He is revolted
by how little of himself he can control.
His hand twitches. He steadies it. Patiently,
it waits for him, revoltingly alone, to be who he is.
An appetite, hungry for submission.

Bird and I stand at the bus stop. As she lights a cigarette, it begins to snow, lightly. I had not finished the laundry, and so Bird rubs her shins together, frictions her palm over where skirt covers thigh. What?, I lean into her. She coughs smoke, which fogs my glasses.

Violate us, Bird, whose most striking feature
is to deprive. It is not hard to
trust, though the consequences are bleaker
when absolute. Really, what love could feature
an endless giving over to another?
As cigarettes give to lung, the lung chars.
Violate what it is you really must strike out
of you. Go ahead, B. Deprive me of what it is hard to.

Fork gleaming in the gaslamp, the Admiral disappears a piece of dewberry pie behind his teeth. After he swallows, he tells Bird, touching her hand the way he's seen people do in similar situations, that he found the man near a violet-leafed bush, nearly suffocated, nearly trembling.

By reason of the insatiability of prayer
everything before him became god.
The world in high voltage—a clinamen flared.
Insatiable, not for reason, but for prayer,
he felt the world like mold blooming in lungs.
Whoever wanted to live, but not completely?
Prayer made him, a hedonist, insatiable for
everything. Salivating salvation. God, to become him.

The noonlight of a cellar door opens on the grit and mold-growth of stone, the way I feel when I wake up, head a bottle of Goldschläger, heart a half-rotted potato.

So, now, half drowning, & bringing a man
of god with me, I was incapable of saving myself,
or anyone. It is luminous—the limits of a life.
Half of what I've inherited—a man. The other—
some part of a person that I can't stand,
something rotted in the back of a cellar shelf.
So bring it out. Boil it. Half drown it in salt.
There's some good. Save, please, the half-dead half.

While living for a time in Montana, Bird and I tried to build a snowman. The pastel blue of morning's promised postcards. But in Butte, the snow, like the lives of the folks that lived there, was too dry. And so we dumped a mug of water on the snow, rolled it a few inches. Dump. Roll. Dump. Roll. Again.

So there I sat—sad shamble of a morning.
It was December. We were used to
doing nothing. Energy is a horrible thing
to have when you are ashamed of the shambles:
your life, the way everything is always boring.
Shame, Bird says, the way, like a balloon, we
go through these shams of flight, tied
to what we're used to. A December of was.

Pulling daisies, frozen at their tips, I glance up from the garden. Bird is sitting at the breakfast nook. She smooches a wine glass and smears the leftover lipstick on the window. I snatch up another flower. Dirt crumbles into a hole I've created. Like sunlight, she maneuvers on a shaft of air, away.

Breath is everywhere. There are no edges.
Inescapably, she moves in love & out of all
silhouettes. A glass of wine on a window ledge,
her behavior is. Everywhere we are. No, edgeless.
Pressed, her lips to rim, rim to pane: twin smudges.
Weather wearing on my skin, I see this, this dirty calling.
Breathe. A flushing. Everywhere is the edge of no.
Inescapably, she moves—out of love, maybe. Or all in.

Haloing the kitchen table, the gaslamp flares on the silverware. Outside, the sun, receding, polishes a spoon on the last lumps of snow.

She can regard all moments as equal and inter-
changeable. So, too, we promise, despite the straitjacket of time.
Who could love someone, she says, who loves
the cold? I took it out, hail & frost, on the hen.
We fry her plucked flesh in lard, welcoming the winter.
So, too, does Bird's mood soften, become brined.
Regards—all moments. Enter each. Equally
the same, though changed. So, too, are we. I promise.

Walking through the light snowfall, I remember the day, a little over a year ago, when the river churned up silt and leaves, and you, strung out by the rain, left for a long time.

We have fallen, I admit. No, Bird, never mind, return
to the lint-dry air upon this one day of the year—
a mirroring, shadows digesting themselves on snow,
impressions of salt and carbon where we have fallen—
staccato of snowfall disturbed by movement through the flakes.
Everything comfortable, shaken. As water is ruffled by trout,
the soil, a gaseous planet, salted, and carbon-drenched, returns
to the riverbed. Dirt meeting its origins of dirt. One day, a year.

Possibly because of the sound silence stuffs into my throat, I wake up. The air is standing water in a basement where the flies waver. Nothing is visible beyond the window's black hole. Bird is somewhere teaching English in Montana. She hates it and I take this as a sign that she wants me. I cough. I wipe sweat from my upper lip. Gasping, hungry for light, and her, I emit this.

The boundary of flesh & self is only suddenly.
Separating the taste for which it longs.
Bird, ravage what it is you judge in me.
Flesh & self. The bonds of only & suddenly.
Lone is to be filled, to yearn. Insatiable, small gifts
of wrong. Sleeping, you are your own only
song. The boundary of flesh is self. Suddenly, only
the longing is separated. Which, a dark window, is you.

2.

Brother,

What follows is an unfinished draft of an essay on the consequences of believing in Romantic Love. The criticism is centered through Malcolm Lowry's *Under the Volcano*, and with this essay, I'd hoped, like most goals of my life, to polish it into a traditionally acceptable form. Literary Criticism specifically and Rhetoric in general have their *moves* one must make—the shapes and shifts of written argument— that I've failed to complete. Thinking about it, now, the expectation of certain moves in writing is not that different from the shifts and shapes expected when enacting the process of what our society defines as "Love": courting, gender roles, grand gestures of jewelry, and small gestures of chocolates.[1] The various mechanisms of an idyllic but ultimately fictitious "Love."

I realize I am the last person who should be lecturing you about love or writing on its practical applications. Given my history, I may lack credibility on the topic. Or maybe I learned something and realized my utter and complete failures, and in my continuous trying to be a better person, I hope to help you avoid different mistakes (as you are more in control of yourself than me), but mistakes, nonetheless.

Consequently, I remain as unfocused here as I do in the essay. My main goal was to outline how the novel's characters became enraptured by the idea of an ever-allusive Romantic Love, and how, in desiring this unattainable state, they had instead found the bitterness of unrealized expectations.[2]

---

1 I admit, Bird, I never bought you chocolates, other than the square bars from the grocery store, which you unwrapped and ate with pleasure on our second-hand couch.

2 The expression on your face as I speak, and me, noting the slight-but-not-full smile, or the narrowing and widening of your eyes, suddenly shifting my tone, or changing my approach all together.

I am sending you these failed fragments in faith that these sketches might aid in your relationship with Bird, as the two of you—but you more than her—often presume a love that doesn't exist. I don't mean that Bird doesn't love you; I mean that your concept of love is an idea lacking physical or practical substance.[3] No one kisses in the fucking rain, brother, and if they do it sure doesn't bring anything other than wet shoes.

I want to provide part of a note about the novel's most pressing frustration for readers. The obvious conundrum of the novel is as follows: Why can't the Consul allow himself to rekindle his relationship with Yvonne and relinquish his self-destructive and alcoholic behavior? These are the main character flaws of Geoffrey "the Consul" Firmin, but this problem opens up another question: Is the Consul's addiction natural, and ingrained in him by the decades in which he is alive, or is he his own failure? Can he refuse drinks, as his own free choice, or has the choice of drinking already been decided and is pathological? In an introduction to the work, Stephen Spender says, "being chosen by one's addiction means also that there is a postponed choice, not in one's own hands, but in one's heart, though unknown to oneself," which you should find familiar, brother, as you should know well that "the choice that decides whether one is dammed in Hell or whether—without one knowing it oneself—one is seeking redemption" (xxv).[4] Thinking on your relationship, I wonder if the two of you could even help yourselves.[5] Not

---

3 We emerged in such a negative state. Not negative as detrimental, but negative as vacuous. The undefined. An edgelessness. As when you snap open a pistachio shell to discover no seed, though this emptiness is rarer than a presence. The rarity of nothing when something is common.

4 Were we seeking, Bird, destruction of ourselves, and our love, to trample them completely, or were we seeking redemption from love entirely and from each other?

5 Not the notes on the chalkboard, Bird, but the leftover and imprinted dust of prior notes.

in the failures alone, but in the moments of tenderness too.[6] I wonder if your character traits, the pathological enactments of your lives, had drawn you towards each other like a cliché—a moth to a flame, an addict to his compulsions, culture to its imitations of art.[7]

This essay, similar to your relationship, is fractured, disjointed, and prone to unexpected shifts of tone and idea. It is lacking transitions and devoid of a full shape. It is seeking out an expected form but fails to find that form. Like your love, it is unfinished, and probably never to be finished.

With love and not Love,

Marcellus, or as you call me, brother, "The Admiral"

---

6 Not in our kindness, no, but in our necessary meanness.

7 Remember, Bird, that picture we took in the wintered field of Montana—you standing on a hay bale, arms spread and raised to the sky? You were announcing your presence with the blinding-but-still-dulled white of winter behind you, and in an error of light or of photographic development, a green and luminous column formed from you to me—a sort of phantom of energy, I said, and in my youth I thought it meant we were connected, though now I know you weren't yelling for me or for us. The breath rising above you was yours.

Consequences and Simulations: Unrealistic Conceptions of Love in Malcom Lowry's *Under the Volcano.*

Love as Illusion

Significant characters in the novel trust in and perform a romanticized, idyllic version of Love.[8] This unfolds not as real love—which we slug through every day in the pains and small joys of those close to us—but as Love as an idea: an unattainable, fictionalized concept.[9]

The novel opens with Jacques Laruelle, after the Consul and Yvonne have been dead a year and as M. Laruelle's departure from Quauhnahuac is clouded by his memories of his time with them and his love for Yvonne. When describing an unexpected rain that soaks his clothes and alerts his consciousness to the ultra-presentness of the moment, M. Laruelle depicts it as a rain that he could "walk on and on through this wild country in his clinging white flannels getting wetter and wetter and wetter" (10). This permeation, the continuousness and the accumulation of the rain and its wetness, he compares to "love which comes too late" (11)—an unexpected Love, one which would annoy most but which M. Laruelle embraces as an experience of life. This, of course, represents a romantic notion of his Love for Yvonne, a Love which causes him immense pain given that she is married to the Consul and that their affair meant more to him than to her. Despite the fanciful comparison of his Love to rain (what is more romantic than walking in it, than kissing

---

8 We walk into a room. We meet each other. There is no context or story for before—we are just there, adjusting, figuring out the new now without knowing where each of us had come from.

9 Us watching John Cusack and Kate Beckinsale reach for the same pair of satin gloves while you hog the popcorn and someone behind me slurps air and ice from their soda-less cup.

in it?), this Love for Yvonne left him soaked, never dried off in the sun, and molded over.[10] It isn't a real love, but one depicted as an idea.

The character most tragically infected by this romantic ideal of Love is Yvonne. She desperately wants her marriage with the Consul to be harmonious, and she is willing to fool herself into believing it can be repaired and can be healthy. This is best represented by her thoughts on their possible future life together. While watching the bull fights in the arena, Yvonne fantasizes about a life and a Love she might have with the Consul if they leave Quauhnahuac together. It becomes increasingly clear, though, that this dream life she plans for them is unrealistic, as the details she ponders are too flowery and fanciful for even a couple in a healthy relationship. For instance, in their hypothetical inhabitance, the house stood between the forest and the shores of the ocean, and from the forest to the shore the path flourished in "salmonberries and thimbleberries and wild blackberry bushes[11] that on bright winter nights of frost reflected a million moons" (279–280). Around their home, they are surrounded by nature and wildlife: "a heron[12], that seemed made of cardboard and string, would flap past heavily" (282). Also, "kingfishers and swallows flitted past the eaves or perched on the pier. Or a seagull would slide past perched on a piece of driftwood, his head on his wing, rocking, rocking with the motion of the sea." In this romanticized, unrealistic life of

---

10 You always talked about the sound of rain, Bird, its closeness and its distance. We listened from inside the room. Light broke over the droplets on the window. Multiply, you said. What a sonically-steeped word. The distance of the word, the closeness of the word in relation to rain—how I felt about separate iterations of our love.

11 A love embodied by picking wild dewberries in a field and turning them into jam. A relationship of spreading sour-sweet purpleness over hot bread.

12 An egret. An owl. Often, two cardinals.

theirs, they also encounter sea creatures: "at half tide they would look down from their pier and see, in the shallow lucid water, turquoise and vermillion and purple starfish, and small brown velvet crabs sidling along barnacled stones brocaded like heart-shaped pincushions." Amongst this nature, somehow, despite his history, the Consul would chop wood as Yvonne cooked, and he would finally work on his long talked-about book, and the book would bring him fame, but neither of them would care about this,[13] as "they would continue to live, in simplicity and in love, in their home between the forest and the sea" (282). The tone of this is dream-like, and the reader can tell that the situation is not realistic, as even loyal, non-toxic relationships fail to live in such an ideal state. Yvonne has, after all, been separated from the Consul for some time, and when she first saw him again, he was at a bar, sockless because the tremors of his alcoholism proved too powerful for him to put on socks. As Yvonne cannot face the truth about her husband and about not only their chances at reconciliation but also about the quality of their lives if they did reconcile, she instead fantasizes of a life so ridiculously perfect as to be a poem. In her frantic attempt to hold onto her marriage, she cannot cling to reality, and must lose herself in this false ideal about her Love and about love itself.[14]

Even the Consul, despite the constant hangover and poor health caused by his alcoholism, and despite his overall sour mood towards his marriage, finds himself seduced by unrealistic ideals of Romantic Love. Though this concept is often linked in our culture to Shakespeare's *Romeo and Juliet* or to poorly written romantic comedies, the Consul references another

---

13 We planted a flowerbed outside our rented house. All morning you dug up weeds and rocks and dry soil. Every so often, dirt on your face, you glared into where I was reading. I wasn't helping, though I knew, as you surely knew, that you were just avoiding your real work or any conversation we might have about it.

14 This is her downfall—believing in a man not to be believed in.

fictional character lost in the insanity of romance. With a reference to Don Quixote, a character who believes in only Romantic Love and not its actual and common occurrences, Geoffrey refers to himself as "The Knight of Sorry Aspect" and claims he is "haunted continuously by the thought of your songs, of your warmth and merriment…the sweet beginning of our marriage" (41). He is haunted[15], as we all are, by the illusion of Love, of tenderness and companionship as a fanciful notion. He knows that this is the only love he can return to, but that since it is fake, he fears it, and fears that he will be duped by it. He is terrified of suffering, at best, more general hardships of a relationship, and, at worst, more cuckoldry and self-shame.

Since Love is a fiction—an artificial replication of real love[16]—, it is natural that we would play a part in this fiction as characters, just as Don Quixote does, just as the Consul and Yvonne do. Yvonne even references this simulation. When she first returns and finds the Consul sitting at the bar, a mentioning of Oaxaca (a town where the Consul fled to after she first left but where they had been happily in love once[17]) pains her at the word's utterance, and in the jolt of this pain she recognizes the Consul is playing separate "parts" for her and the bartender. It reads, "She was watching the Consul who seemed less on the defensive than in process while straightening out the leaflets on the bar of changing mentally from the part played for Fernando to the part he would play for her" (51). To live in the various and shifting fictions of our lives, we must enact the characters of these fictions, and we must be able to switch our emphasis

---

15 He is haunted by the white night gowns of human connection.

16 Like when you used your grandmother's recipe for pralines but used so much sugar they were inedible.

17 To find, as we do, that memory shapes the event—that all that's happened to us after has recolored our remembrance, so we no longer desire the original but rather the rehued version.

or enactments. The consequences of this, for love, though, can be disastrous.[18]

The Consul, too, recognizes this idea of playing a part, as he thinks of Love as some simulation or imitation of prior iterations in literature.[19] As the consul reads some of the letters Yvonne sent to him during their separation, he thinks, regarding the letters, that Yvonne must have been "reading *something*" while writing these letters, and he thought she had possibly been reading *The Letters of Abelard and Héloïse*. He thinks this type of love must be positioned in language, that it is not a true iteration of life but a copy of fictions. He cannot imagine love outside of a replication of art and ideas.[20]

Toxic Enactments of Love

Love expected and enacted as a romantic ideal ends in disillusionment, heartbreak, bitterness—the disappointment of our lives not meeting our desires.

The Consul admits this more than any of the other characters, and that is why he never sends any of the letters written in response to Yonne's letters. In one such unsent letter, the Consul pleads for Yvonne's help in not Loving her, in extinguishing his Love for her, and he admits that without her help, he may

---

18 Men with flowers. Men in shirts with pressed collars. Men with rough hands. Men who understand. Men who love from a distance. Men who take charge. Men who are cheated on. Men who wash dishes. Men who forgive.

19 Women who expect flowers. Women who wait for walks and hands held. Women who leave. Women who plant their own flowerbeds. Women who suffer infidelity. Women who fold sheets. Women who come back.

20 How often had we acted out, unconsciously, our favorite poems, the scenes from movies we'd admired, the embodiments of characters that we'd read. It makes me wonder if any part of our interactions had been authentic—or is that just life, a replication of all we've seen and heard and read?

relapse back into the toxic and harmful Love they share. He says, "If I am to survive, I need your help. Otherwise, sooner or later, I shall fall" (39).[21] The Consul's answers to Yvonne's letters, then, and his guarding against falling back in Love with her, is to simply refuse to send her any letters in response. Of course, he struggles with this decision, as he does write responses that he never sends.[22] He knows that if he allows himself to, he will fall back into the toxic enactments of a fictionalized Love, which will only end in more heartache.[23]

Despite Yvonne's attempts at reconciliation, the two of them cannot help each other, which is why the novel ends as it does—with Yvonne trampled and the Consul shot and thrown in the ditch like a dog. They cannot find in each other any real comforts, let alone their misguided notions of Love. This is why, in one of the letters the Consul never sent to Yvonne, he says,

> "Endlessly haunted waking and sleeping by the thought that you may need my help, which I cannot give, as I need yours, which you cannot, seeing you in visions and in every shadow, I have been compelled to write this, which I can never send, to ask you what we can do" (42).

The two care for each other, yes, but they aren't good for each other. They believe in false notions of Love, and when the

---

21 "If, Bird, would like a blight/ memory, or you, our love,/ reimagined as decay"—this is a fragment of a poem I abandoned, Bird. I felt it too much, like your flowerbed now overrun with weeds, and there are too many decays, anyway, to list.

22 But we know, Bird, that a non-response takes more energy than a response, as its efforts compound on themselves daily—the choice of not taking action; the more exhausting choice.

23 With my belongings packed into my car, I turned around, after a few blocks, to find you wailing on the bed, and I barely spoke for the burning in my lungs and throat, though I managed to say, "But I do love you." It hung there. "I love you. Isn't that enough?" It started to emulsify. I know now that your failure to respond was a kindness to both of us.

dream breaks, the everyday comforts and connections of real companionship cannot overcome their disconnections.[24]

The Consul does not confine his non-responses to only letters, though, as he thinks but does not verbally respond to Yvonne's pleading for tenderness and clarity. When Yvonne asks the Consul in person, "Haven't you got any tenderness or love left for me at all?" the Consul thought:

> Yes, I do love you, I have all the love in the world left for you, only that seems so far away from me and so strange too, for it is as though I could almost hear it, a droning or a weeping, but far, far away, and a sad lost sound. It might be either approaching or receding, I can't tell which. (206)[25]

The Consul's lack of clarity, straightforwardness, or response to Yvonne is a serious cruelty, as he keeps her guessing and hoping and believing in Love. It also causes miscommunications, as Yvonne thinks his mind is on alcohol here, and not on their relationship.[26] The Consul knows the burden and power he carries; he knows he can forgive Yvonne and bring some sense of understanding and kindness into their lives, but he refuses.

---

24 The Consul and Yvonne have rejected, Bird, as we did, the real textures of love, which are not poems and which are not songs and which are not letters or endings to movies, but which are smaller moments in a life—your snotty tissues on the side of the bed, us running out of gas on the highway, the time barely anyone came to my reading and so I looked and read for you alone in that coffee shop with the glasses clinking and chairs shuffling and my voice on the page projected towards you and not always you.

25 Love like a gong, struck and reverberating: still felt, still thrumming, though the vibrations are receding. Until I'm frail I'll feel this same chord of once was.

26 Misunderstandings of the fictions we enact—Love, Kindness, Cultural Values—are where conflicts reside, Bird, as we are looking at the same phenomenon but through different lenses, both expecting results from a shared understanding that doesn't exist. This is true of you, of me, of all of us.

He even admits that his forgiveness will help them reconcile, but he cannot do it, as he feels "this urgent desire to hurt, to provoke at a time when forgiveness alone could save the day" (207). The Consul, of course, cannot bring himself to this forgiveness or compassion, and so their Love never settles into a realistic, complex, and textured love of contentment—one which acknowledges pain and places it alongside the daily comforts of a partner.[27]

Though Yvonne is the character most infected[28] by Romantic Love, she abandons her fantasies of an idyllic life with the Consul only after all is lost. After the consul leaves the Salon Ofelia where he, Yvonne, and his brother, Hugh, had been drinking, he signals to the reader and to himself of his inability to truly get over his marital troubles. As Yvonne and Hugh search for him, a storm starts up, and Yvonne, tragically, is trampled by a riderless horse (the same horse that startles off when the Consul is shot dead). As the horse stomps over her, and as she lies dying, she envisions the house of her dreams— the house between the sea and the forest, her "rebirth" with her husband—on fire. Everything is burning down. This signals, finally, and too late for her, that she recognizes her misguided and naïve hopes for her marriage.[29]

So we come back to the question, why can't the Consul rekindle with Yvonne and abandon his self-destructive behavior and alcoholism? Some would argue, as Spender does, that the Consul "rejects love to protect [his] isolation,"[30] something he

27 Love is not a flower, bright but bound to wilt, but a succulent, half-shade, half-light, little water.

28 The virus of ideas—the replication of a meme. Love as a viral replication of art.

29 When did each of us, in our own hour, not in the receding but in the humidity-filled heat of mid-day, admit this to ourselves?

30 It was probably over, finally, when you no longer cared if I came to bed with you, but contentedly fell asleep while I stayed up reading and writing.

considers to be "his deepest truth" (xvii). For instance, after the consul returns home from passing out in the middle of the road, nearly getting himself run over, Yvonne mentions the possibility of her and the Consul leaving together, but the Consul is horrified by this enactment of forgiveness and reconciliation:

> "*Now?*" he found he had said gently. "But we can't very well go away *now* can we, what with Hugh and you and me and one thing and other, don't you think? It's a little unfeasible, isn't it?" (For his salvation might not have seemed so large with menace had not the Burke's Irish whiskey chosen suddenly to tighten, if almost imperceptibly, a screw. It was the soaring of this moment, conceived of as continuous, that felt itself threatened. (87)

He is terrified by the idea of a disruption of his isolation and his decay. He does not want salvation, is never going to forgive Yvonne her infidelities, is never going to give up drinking or act in a way where their love could return. But why?[31]

On the idea of leaving, the Consul tells a story someone told someone he knew,[32] though he recalls it as if it happened to him.[33] In the story, he travels to different towns, but they're all the same, and the Consul ends his rambling, disjointed anecdote by saying, "What's the use escaping...from ourselves?" (88). The answer, for the Consul, of course, is that there is no use. The problem isn't in the place or the particular moment in time, but in their inherent characters—you can't outrun yourself, and you can't hide yourself in romantic fantasies of Love passed down from Shakespeare and the Abelard and Héloïse letters. What Yvonne wants to call a "rebirth," the Consul views as

---

31 In my writing I have naively hoped, if not to answer, then to find this reconciliation.

32 In the act of loving, we tell a story someone told someone we knew.

33 Our mistake that it could or is happening to us.

an "escape," and their discrepancies on how they embody this difference leads to tragedy for both of them.

The obstacles to pleasure, the sorrows and melancholy of the book, our interactions in the dense, layered language, are to show that thought and consciousness—humanity—are obstacles to contentment, not only in themselves but in the fictions they create, such as "Love," which can never be fully realized. What can one do, though, but carry on?

3.

Slouching in a scrap of grass near an abandoned gas station, Bird found a book, half weather-worn, its cover torn. She began to paraphrase from page eighty-seven. Palimpsests, I said, noticing the reflections of cars, passing along highway 216, on the station's empty window.

The lovers believe they are inventing love.
What other trope do they need?
Bird, nearer the earth, giving herself. Shadowed above,
I am the meaning she believes the sun erases. Love,
she says, ruffling dress over knees, is not enough.
What happens after we, rewritten, feed on
the intentions the lovers believed in? Then, they are
some other simulation. Not of need, no no, but of you?

Bird began salvaging a pile of plucked chives near the roadway. I leaned back on my elbows. Wind dissipated a flock of dust a truck kicked up. When the dust cleared, a robin, nesting in an abandoned car, blessed the road-light.

The bird was coming back, a robin maybe, or oh god, yes,
here, here, out of nowhere, believe me. She was coming
through the pollen-plagued window, feathers dark soot, dressed
as a bird would coming back from god-knows-what, saying yes,
yes, here, here, out of nowhere, come: believe me
before everything, or nothing—who knows?—remains,
before the rest of the birds, squalor in their lungs, return.
Here, here, out of nowhere. Yes. She was coming to believe in us.

Days strung out in pastels, canapés, the dust of a
veranda.

Eat? I should eat. So, stomach a gutted balloon, the Admiral
eats a half a canapé. Like his life, the sunlight settles. He doesn't know
the weight of light, how much dust must be between the Adderall
in his stomach & the soft spot on his gums. The Admiral
posturing in the sunlight of the veranda, fingers crumbed, admiring
the shamelessness of a cat preening itself on a rowboat,
the cat choosing to lick the bird-dust especially for his Highness
who, having eaten half a canapé, clueless, couldn't say no.

Sitting in the window booth of the City Café, I ignored the way Bird was folding her paper placemat into a crane by looking at my slight reflection. Across the street, a child, holding his rolled up jacket like a stuffed animal, was being forced into the backseat of a station wagon filled with boxes. The license plate read from way out of state.

Perhaps because they don't have home towns, just places
where they were born. Hollyhocks—the backyards
of Missoula, Mobile, Tuscaloosa. An array of spaces
they can't call home, perhaps because they can't place towns
like these into any one area of their lives—a blur of basements,
kitchens, the small dirt lots where the earth is hard.
Doesn't the world, perhaps, have towns that are just places
where hollyhocks are born? The back of all backyards?

Because the day was nice, we decided to lunch in a meadow where we could see the forest. The trees, in the dry air, inched towards us, then quivered back—the lips of a Venus fly trap. Sections of them had browned from the damages that the pine beetle, half-hungry, like us, inflicted. Sections of them, waiting to be burned.

Because what, after all, is so wrong with now?
We had prolonged the world a little while at least.
The Admiral, drunk, ruffled a hankie into his collar, gave a bow.
After all, is it so wrong? And because of what? Now,
Bird said, but air, smelling of moldy grass, whiffed out.
The world should be set aside awhile in its glass case.
After all, is now so wrong? Could it be we made,
like the world, that little thing, at least, a prolonged mistake?

Bird and I, on a blanket in the yard, face the road. She cradles a glass of water with a lemon in it neither of us has touched. The sun pelts when the wind does not and her glass slowly sweats. Not a car, not even a bicycle, rustles up dust.

To gather all other moments into itself.
The ambiguities of always wanting.
Us, struck as such. Even lasting has a shelf
life. Gathered of all moments. Itself
also wanting the lack which time brings. Help
me consider, Bird, why to continue is so daunting.
Why staring into the roadkill of all moments is
itself ambiguous. Wanting always to be not wanting.

After spending three days drinking from someone else's well, the Admiral became very sick—sheets smelling like the well's stone sides, mouth tasting of the moss that grows there. As I walk through an orchard near the water pump, thinking of his insistence on self-dependence, I see, in the tree, a plum large as a baby's head. The next day, I pull Bird away from where she is nursing the Admiral. The plum has fallen and appears eaten from the inside. Time, not in anytime, really, the Admiral whispering, *This is what my life is.*

But where is the sense of loss? What a very
weighted moment to have fallen. A plum gorged
from the inside—to collapse is all I ask for.
But what's the point? To be lost is to nearly
never exist at all. Though to hold on is clearly
not worth losing friends over. A worm forged
just under the skin—the sensation is very
heavy. Finding, momentarily, what loss isn't.

As I limp to the river on a trail we'd made by pressing into the same earth for several years, I sleeve through some low hanging willow limbs and see Bird turning from the shoreline, the light of her lantern like little stars on the water bugs, then the light burning them out, and the water blackening, and her face caught by it so that I can distinguish, in her horror at seeing me there, her remorse.

Where she does most damage to herself,
then the metaphor's at its most useful.
Charred by her own propulsion. What else
she does, where she damages, her self
only knows how much warmth is felt
by the gas. Before she burns there, or after.
Where she does mostly put herself is damaged
in the light. Mostly a meteor, unsighted.

The Admiral told me this story: As the roar of the other children whipped through the brush, he snapped back his slingshot, launching a rock at a cedar tree. From shook branches, a bird flapped for a few erratic feet, then fell. What the Admiral witnessed when he looked in its eyes— the same thing in his wife's eyes every night, before she died, as he undid the buttons of his longjohns.

Whatever he felt—fear, guilt, shame, love, grief—he was alone with his own appetites. A taxidermied pheasant only half stuffed is what he felt like. The shame & guilt of love. Of considering something because you can hold it long enough to realize it doesn't want whatever love you felt—fear & shame, mostly guilt. Alone in his grief. Pity, an appetite.

Because Bird hated Montana, and I went there to testify to her discomfort, we moved back to Alabama. We've been here awhile. In small grey cotton shorts she hangs a strip of sticky paper above the kitchen tiles, the paper turning over, shining bright, then black on its backside. Sweat micas her neck. I reach for her and for a moment I believe—because I feel that she will leave again soon—that I shouldn't touch her.

We cannot really say what desire is
to bring absence into presence, or to collapse
some comfort in which we've conspired.
Bird, say what you cannot really. What desire
would drive you this way? A raptus, fly paper
that somehow, on its sticky strip, trapped
a desire we cannot really say. Some plump bug.
Is a collapse always so present in your absence?

Lungs stuffed with dried paper, Bird and I sit down
begin to eat a meal. She worries the tablecloth's fringe
end. A shadow, like a cigarette flicked from a passing car
hits the window—the only movement of the afternoon

But the world, rainwater roiled in gasoline, goes forward—
dust in a Buick's heater vent, harvest moon, hands of exhausted survivors—
Bird & I, vapors of an oilless engine, sitting at the kitchen table, bored
of the world. Silence an oven our heads are closed in. She goes forward
with what she needs to tell me, tongue a spark plug. I've heard
it all, kerosene-weary—the world, her words,
scraps, burnt sand, spent matches in the hands of exhausted survivors.

Standing in front of the garbage dump, I pluck a smooth stone from the ground and offer it to Bird. She feels its weight in her hand, turning it over, then throws it. When it lands, the pigeons, like doves at a wedding, flock to the sky. The sun behind them red from smog. Coughing, Bird believes this lift is an omen, and she steps inside the gate. In the mud she finds a Barbie. One arm is missing. The dress is browned, ragged, torn so that a nipple-less boob is exposed. Someone has burnt her hair, which mats, like hope, to her scalp.

The idea of a woman having to have a single pure life
is how the Admiral was raised. Our mother, her mother, etc.
So he couldn't explain why his wife
drove into the pond: "Women are the ideal of a simple purity."
The shape aimed for only attained through suffering,
surgery, liposuction, little girls with plastic lips, & pale shins.
The idea: "Her life was simple. She never left the house."
How the Admiral raised this as a question, etc.

I offer my arm to her, wondering if the scent, salty like mushrooms, is from her perfume or my sweat. She sighs. Sunlight, rising in, flaps through the curtains and preens there. Bird picks her dress up from the hardwood. As she sweeps the dust from its daisy pattern, she hums the word *aubade* until she's gone.

Of the sunlight, sifting to pale, fine dust.
A rooster's song—a lawn mower in the heart.
There seems no way for you & I, though we
must shift in the pale, fine dust of the sunlight.
Quiet is the curtain she can't stand. How can I trust,
I say, you'll be back? This is, Bird says, such a ragged
fine rust, you & I. Sunlight sifting through. Pale,
Bird's chord in the heart. A lawnmower, a scythe.

At a rest stop, several days in, I sit in grass still damp from the day's showers. I smell the mulch of wind through trees. No leaves are falling. Bird, standing on a picnic bench, trumpets a sparkler around, its light shifting: red, yellow, blue. Its light visible only for me.

& then we said nothing else, staring ahead at the road,
or off to the side where miles of trees had been burned.
A single sparkler is a promise of mushrooms. We unloaded
the nothing we carried. What else did we have but road,
the taste of charcoal on our teeth? We should've known
nothing would come of our decision to turn
in the nothing we owned for what might be ahead,
or far off, to the side, miles up, burning—of everywhere.

Placed in the sun of the bedroom window for so long, the cloth of a suitcase, open, but never packed, begins to lighten in color.

There is no wind to carry, bear, or even refuse
to bear a sound so heavy as regret.
We go about the echoes of our lives as if we choose
the windless bearings of our hearts. Please, Bird, refuse
the light nudge of my toes on your calves in the morning,
the way the silverware is always only half set.
There is no wind. Not for you. Only the refusal you bear
so heavy, but regret to bear. An echo: a sound unheard.

Algae dripping from his hat, face soaked to hide his crying, the Admiral pulls several pieces of folded-up paper from the pocket of his shirt. On the floor near the heater, he lays them out, as if maps to a place he could never emotionally afford to travel to.

I have not forgotten the Mazepine or the pressed violets.
The garden in Bessemer where he strolled into the lake fully clothed.
The Admiral, waking with minnows in his beard, wrote triolets
I have not forgotten. The Mazepine, he said, at the present, violates
what's defined in this light. The window where a hummingbird pilots,
he hid the curtains over. His shirt from the night before had begun to mold.
I have not forgotten, he said, voice wet gunpowder, the present, violent as it is.
Bird had removed every rock. Fully clothed, into the lake, again, he strolled.

As I float down the creek, rocks scrape my back. The smoke of my cigarette—still, amazingly, lit—drifts over me, then disappears, opening up the sky.

Callused cartilage, a blocked artery—her yearning.
Exceeded, but never relieved, by fulfillment.
A river, choked with trash asked for, now burning
for space. Callous, this constant yearning for her.
A match hitting water, water hitting sky—as smoke.
The smoke's only worth: covering up dead stars.
Pumped through the arteries of every person—a yearning
never fulfilled. Only excessively relieved. If that.

The night after a rare snow-sighting in Alabama, Bird trots through the lawn's slosh. She opens her mouth to chant, but instead swallows a spark from a nearby bonfire. "Is it?" she asks. "What?" I forgot to put on shoes, and so my socks are wet. "Follow me," she says, gesturing, like a magician's assistant, at her throat.

The end of the world, and the beginning, and the waste
in between. Snowflakes falling & drying on pavement.
Despite clear roads, I shouldn't have to face
the end or the beginning of the world—a waste
of energy. Someone should. I fold my shirts, slowly.
Some of them have bleach stains. Some of them, lint.
The waste at the beginning is at an end. The world
in between dying. Snowflakes, breaklights, pavement.

As the Admiral fiddles with the valve on a kerosene lamp, the skin of his face passes from lighter to darker, creases becoming clearer, disappearing. He snaps off the light, shrugs phlegm through his throat, and says, *I wish my— hmm—life was like that.*

The fragment of history is to foreclose
then upon now. You cannot want that, & yet
you do. The past passed over. Suppose
history fragmented is closed & only for
the ones who forget forgetting, those
somnambulists, you & me. Timeline a fretted
history. A fragment of what it is to foreclose
now & then. Ripped wallpaper you can't mend.

The moon is blocked by the Admiral's waving hand as he leans on the railing of the train's platform, the train chugging, like a heart, away from us.

To name anything is to neutralize it enough,
the marker for measuring nostalgia.
If I call it something else, I won't despise it.
Neutralized in the name of how it's stifled,
a room filled with people so you can't leave,
the river you step in so cold it's burning
your blood. Enough, the name you call yourself,
measuring remorse by the man marked: waving & away.

Because Bird's side of the bed is only wrinkled
sheets now, I take a stroll through the alleys.
Sunlight, not choked by smoke, is a golden grey,
an unstrung sonata, all I can hope for.

To make, or utter in, short, shrill tones,
as some birds do, if we believe the bird
sounds not the bird sound. But rather, unalone,
wants to make another utter in short, shrill tones.
I did, last night, into the phone
and listened to how, reverberating back, my words
were made: uttered in shorter, shriller tones
than one bird does, if we believe the bird.

Thinking she could save the petals, Bird fills a vase with cider.

Some blue flowers like forget-me-
nots that had somehow found a place to grow
pale and flaccid in a cider-filled vase on your vanity.
Some blueness flowers like forget me,
Bird, I cannot bear to be
dust scuffed in lungs you must morningly wheeze.
The knots that somehow found a place to grow
in your throat, blue flowers, like, forget it, Bird, forget me.

Leaning against the sliding-glass' frame, just before the grocery store parking lot, where, moments ago I didn't have enough money to buy the bag of lima beans needed for soup, I feel the fabricated air behind, its ventilators screeling, and the sticky air in front, like I am about to walk into a giant's mouth.

I feel purged & holy, ready for a new life.
The sunlight is clear & windless, almost hot.
Receipts, in pocket, balled from the washer. Strife
is simply to be purged, a new life, more holy.
The vinegar in our hearts, lungs a gutted pig—
an illusion. The only absolute truth needed is
to not. Purged, & holy. I feel ready. A new life—
windless & clear. Its sun, hot, almost alight.

4.

Dear J

A snow owl flew from the field beside me today, and as it spread its wings, it imprinted on the snow's crust an impression of its breast and wingspan. Feathers etched, like the connotations of words, on the drift. The snow was still falling, rather heavily, and I stood and watched as this bright imprint of the bird's athletic form slowly blurred. Eventually, the tundra covered it. It reminded me of us—the sharp etchings of our life together that ended so abruptly. In our separation, filled in with everything else one does with their life, I have been reading *The Letters of Abelard and Héloïse*, and been thinking about their brief love—how Héloïse wrote to Abelard after a long separation; how love of a different and more lasting note can form from parting.

What is the texture of love, other than memory, salt, the fragrance of a room we have long been absent in?

As I read these letters, I wanted to talk about us—to you, yes, but through you to myself—and about the general kinship and kind I felt with Héloïse, not because our situations were similar, but because I, like you, like us, understand the shifts and reforming of a relationship over time, especially one spent apart and one remembered. Through this letter, like her letters, I wanted to talk about us, to you, though you are not here, which makes you the perfect audience to hear me out.

I remember you reading, one afternoon, a ratty, second-hand copy of this book, the pages wavy from water and musty from sitting in a stack in your closet. You dropped three dried dandelion florets into a mug of steaming water and read the pages of the book as you waited for your tea to settle. You said I might like it, since I was learning French, though I never got around to reading it until these many years later. These are my thoughts on the book, which you may see, or which you may throw away unread, but which carry with me always the weight of what I once considered our failed time together. I have now come to understand it as the necessary precursor to our separate, not exactly happy but maybe content lives. Our relationship was like the first full draft of a novel, which having set down and returned to later, became the propulsion for a vastly revised, newer and different story. To get back to it, here are my thoughts on *The Letters*. Part of me wishes you were here to talk to about them in person; part of me is glad you're not; the simultaneous wanting and not wanting is a third energy, more realistic, more organic—nothing better sums up our dynamic than the synergy of these competing feelings.

Like the idea of love itself, certain critics have focused on the romantic and astonishing materials in these letters, and they have ignored or qualified the ugliness of Abelard's behavior and personal values—his predatory acts, his bigotry, his disgust with the female body. Our remembrance of these letters, like our culture's conception of love itself, focuses heavily on the romantic and the spectacular. This is misguided, J. Rather than love, I would have us display a prolonged kindness. Shouldn't we say, instead, not that we are *in love*, but that we are *in kind*? Not that we *can't* be apart, but that we *can* last a separation. Not that you *are* my light, but that you *do not* disturb my light? Make room for it, there, beside your own.

Remember that time I stood on that haybale in Montana. It was dusk, the land snowy but still and the sky muted from the cold. I stood above you on the bail and roared upwards into the sky, you beside me as your mom captured the moment with her camera. In the photo, a green aura developed between us, probably the result of poor film. We said this visible energy meant that we were connected, since it touched between both of us—but I now know what it was: my energy, my aura, spreading out from me, and you there, beside me, allowed to be a part of it. We misunderstood the meaning of it, that green discoloration, and imprinted on it what we wanted to believe, that we were meant to be together—a silly notion borne of a misguided idea about what love can do for two separate people.

Women, in love, and in talking about love, are often mis-understood or misrepresented.

Certain scholars thought the letters as forgiveness, since they couldn't imagine a nun or medieval woman saying such sex-positive things, proud pagan as she was (as you are). As critics held up Abelard and Héloïse's love as ideal, they imagined her as a trope of love, and for the ages they wanted her to be conventionally unconventional, a manufactured and containable version of unbridled love. They did this, of course, not for her sake, but to protect Abelard's reputation, and to erase reference to him as a predator. They hoped to place the couple's love where they are comfortable with it being—as a fiction. We allow for the beautiful and ideal in art, and mistake this for life.

You brought this idea up while we were driving along the Gulf. Bryan Adam's "Summer of '69" came on the radio, and you ranted about the irresponsibility of art of this kind, how people wanted to live in these unattainable mirages of moments. People, you said, like to believe they could live in a manufactured perfection—of their lives in high school, like the song, but also of other imitations of life produced by art. But for all this talk, you failed to understand how you were doing the same for our relationship and our love.

Heloise believed in and argued for a "disinterested love," free of obligations and gains outside of the desire for the other person—J, a love bound by anything but the other's company is not love, but a transaction. Love as economics; companionship as commodity; practice as ideology.

I have come to regard silence and solitude not as an emptiness, but as a fullness of self. The quietude of an indi-vidual being spread out and fulfilling its promise, free from constraints or the selfish hunger of another's being beside me. When you left the house, I felt a mental noise leave as well, as if the room now allowed my own thoughts to per-meate our thrift-store furniture and too-old carpet. Others feel comfortable in the commotion of communion, in the chemical friction of other bodies beside them always. But that was never me, never us, really, as I know you loved your "alone time" also. These years that you have been gone have been a lasting calm. I was always meant to be myself, for me, and some people would call that selfish, but those who do lack empathy and fail to realize a person's sense of purpose outside of their own cravings of constant affirmations from others.

Héloïse, too, entered monastic life, and for twelve years Abelard responded to her sacrifice with silence. I planted, with my father, a fig tree, and watched for twelve years as it grew, in winter through summer, its continual shape both forward and cyclical, sprouting, upward, leaves shedding to new growth, and I imagine now, though I have no reason to, Héloïse also planting a tree her first year at the monastery, watching it grow in isolation as the man she bore a son for never wrote, never visited. What loneliness, and what self-assurance, for her to thrive as she did.

Is Héloïse a woman so famous she needs no last name, like Madonna, or a woman so neglected she was never given one?

Our relationship wasn't much like there's, and neither of us were as despicable as Abelard, but he can't be avoided when talking about *The Letters*.

Abelard was a predator, a rapist, and a racist, though it seems he felt remorse, later in life, for his shameful behavior. For his century, he was a man possessed by logic, who craved its structure and let it rule his life, and who, against his life's work, fell into illogical passion for another. Some would call this love, I guess—the chaos and confusion of romance. Really, he was just a fraud. Though Abelard took years to write to Héloïse, he wrote a letter to an imaginary monk confessing his misfortunes, and this, as you know, solidifies most of the myth of his life. A fictionalized life written to a fictional monk. Despite years of critics romanticizing their relationship, it is hard to think of Abelard as anything other than a predator, someone who sought out Héloïse to groom her as his pupil and who openly admitted to using violence to manipulate her. If this doesn't sum up Western societies psychologically damning enactments and beliefs in "Romantic Love," I don't know what else would. Abelard was a coward and a fraud, not for rejecting Héloïse, as humans constantly reproach and injure each other emotionally, but his shortcomings lie in why he reproached her. In this, he sought the ideals of a philosopher—to live out the concept of a theologian and a thinker, the same bodies of thought which later mythologizes their relationship as a lasting ideal of romance.

The world would be a better place if more men were castrated.

I mention him not because you are like him, but because you believed the romantic ideals that perpetuated out of his and other writings of the time. While we were together, you believed in the artificial trappings of love as theory, and I really have yet to decide if you believed in it as theory itself, or as theory as practiced. Were you Don Quixote never actually trying to find his Dulcinea? Or were you Don Quixote chasing after windmills?

The consequences are the same, either way.

Héloïse speaks of how her and Abelard only faced repercussions after their marriage, a sham marriage, as their bond in its truest form existed outside those bonds—both before, in their carnal connections, and after, in their long-distance letters. Ironically, Héloïse's letters inspired the practice of "courtly love," a concept as literary trope but later enacted as a game. Her correspondence also served as a model for the epistolary game. Only men could take something so profound, personal, and authentic and turn it into a fiction so damaging it would help ensnare men and women for centuries. Love is not marriage, J, but an authenticity of feelings towards another, and in its bodily form, it is dangerous, but in its separation and modification it is lasting and capable of longevity. That is how I see our love, as something that needed to settle, like mountains settling into sand on the beach, like the snowdrift stilling as the wind dies down, like dandelion tea releasing enough of its heat to drink—as individually, each of us in our own separation, in our own way. Something we will carry separately, in our own kind and for our own sake.

Women, as you have admitted to me before, carry most of the weight of this—both its burdens and its redemptions. And after everything, it is Héloïse who brought Abelard's body to be prepared for burial at the Convent of Paraclete. It would have to be, as these moments of love are, both a tenderness and a relief, a giving over and a giving up of love—to be done with you, in grief, to be done with you, in love.

I don't know if you every looked into the events of their life outside of the art of their letters, but I thought you'd find this interesting. Their bodies remain buried beside one another, having been displaced, like their love, several times, now in a cemetery of Père Lachaise. There, if passing by, if visiting, if you know of them and of the different textures and tones of their relationship, you can place a flower, or song, or prayer on their graves. Or you can, as is more appropriate, pass on by in silence and separation.

Heloise ends her first letter "farewell, my only love," and so I will end this one: farewell, my once loved.

In kind,

Bird

NOTES

The refrain lines for most of the triolets are adapted from Malcolm Lowry's *Under the Volcano* (1947) and Anne Carson's *Eros the Bittersweet* (1986). Others are borrowed from Toni Morrison's *The Bluest Eye* (1970), Lorrie Moore's *Who Will Run the Frog Hospital?* (1994), and Sylvia Plath's *The Bell Jar* (1963).

ACKNOWLEDGMENTS

I would like to thank the editors of the following journals, in which some of the poems, in various forms, first appeared: *Indiana Review, Drunken Boat, South Florida Poetry Journal, 2River View, Bear Review, Tule Review, ucity review, Hiram Poetry Review, Caesura, The Odd Magazine,* and *Ginosko Literary Journal.*

"Haloing the kitchen table" appeared in Black Lawrence Press's anthology *Feast: Poetry and Recipes for a Full Seating at Dinner.*

"When the pond water is too brown to see the birds," "Pulling daisies," and "Leaning against the sliding-glass' frame" appeared in the artist's book *Earthwards,* released by Curly Head Press & Bindery.

Thank you, William Broussard, Adam Clay, Thomas Cotsonas, AB Gorham, Lisa Tallin, and Danilo Thomas for being my friends in life and in literature. Also, Sonja G. Rossow, for finding a space for my words in your art.

I'm grateful to Nikki Ummel and LMNL arts for supporting my work and for fostering the writing community around New Orleans. I'm also grateful to my many teachers who helped me experiment: Joel Brouwer, Debra Magpie Earling, Joanna Klink, Peter Streckfus, and Robert Stubblefield. A special thanks to Robin Behn for introducing me to the triolet form. Thank you, Dr. Taylor Byas and Brad Richard, for your kind words and your readings.

My eternal thanks to Dr. Ross K. Tangedal, Lillian Kulbeck, Sam Bjork, McKenna Bartel, Gwen Goetter, and everyone on the Cornerstone team for your insights and efforts.

To my family, always, for supporting me, and especially to my wife, Keosha, for everything.

JESSE DELONG is the author of *The Amateur Scientist's Notebook* (2021). He works as the Assistant Director of Creative Writing at Louisiana State University where he teaches writing and literature. Other work has appeared in *Colorado Review, Mid-American Review, Indiana Review,* and *Typo* as well as the anthologies *Best New Poets 2011* and *Feast: Poetry and Recipes for a Full Seating at Dinner.* He lives in Louisiana with his wife, Keosha, and his daughter, Alora.